Lawler Education → *Literacy Matters*

Skills for Literacy 1

Dr Susan Young

Skills for Literacy 1

LAWLER
EDUCATION

Dr Susan Young

The author's rights have been asserted.

© 2018 GLMP Ltd All Rights Reserved.

978-1-84285-455-6

Series Editor: Dr Graham Lawler

Produced and Published by Lawler Education

Lawler Education
Lon Ffawydd/Beech Lane
Abergele
LL22 7DY
www.graham-lawler.com
Lawler Education is a division of GLMP Ltd
and is not affiliated, endorsed or sponsored by any external organisation.

Copyright Notice
The copyright of this book grants the right for one tutor at one provider site to photocopy the activities.
A Multi-User Licence must be purchased for each additional tutor using the same resource at the same site.
Additional Multi-User licences can be purchased at any time.
For providers with multiple sites, each site is treated as an independent site and the above paragraph applies.
The ongoing supply of these materials depends on tutors' professional good judgment and compliance with copyright law. This resource is covered by UK and European copyright law, and CLA polices its use.

You acknowledge in the use of this resource that you are applying your own professional judgement in determining the suitability of the goods for any particular purpose. Neither the publisher nor any/all of their agents can be held accountable for outcomes with students as a result of usng this resource. Teachers should review the resource in the light of their knowledge of their determination of the needs of their student.

Skills for Literacy 1

Number/General Thinking Series
Introducing Algebra 1: Number Patterns and Sequences
Introducing Algebra 2: Specialising and Generalising
Introducing Algebra 3: Introducing Equations
Introducing Algebra 4: Equations and Graphs
Number Machines
Number and Place Value
Entry Level: Writing and Forming Numbers
Multiplication and Division Year 2

Emotional Well Being and Health
Choose Happiness
The Eat Well Stay Slim Budget Cookbook
Write Yourself Well

English/Literacy
Creativity through Language 1: How to Teach Fictional Writing
Creativity through Language 2: How to Teach Informative/Non-Fictional writing
Cloze
Cloze: Cars and Transport
Year 3-4 Crosswords
More Year 3-4 Crosswords

Guided Reading and Writing
More Guided Reading and Writing

Reading for Comprehension 1
Reading for Comprehension 2
Reading for Comprehension 3
Reading for Comprehension 4

Writing and Forming Letters

Writing in Everyday Life Book 1: Making Inferences
Writing in Everyday Life Book 2: Travelling
Writing in Everyday Life Book 3: Asking Questions
Writing in Everyday Life Book 4: Messages

Skills for Literacy 1
Skills for Literacy 2
Skills for Literacy 3
Skills for Literacy 4
Skills for Literacy 5
Skills for Literacy 6
Skills for Literacy 7
Skills for Literacy 8

History
Active Lives 1
Active Lives 2

Cross Curricular
Titanic: The Story of a Tragedy

Financial Literacy/Capability
Back to the Black for Primary Schools
Back to the Black: How to Get Out of Debt and Stay Out of Debt
Understanding the Numbers: The First Steps in Managing Your Money

Understanding Maths

www.graham-lawler.com

Many more titles in development

The ballroom dancing photo p 9, courtesy of Caragius

Teacher Feedback Opportunity

£20 Lawler Education Voucher for detailed and complete reviews. The purpose of this form is to give you, the teacher, an opportunity for improvement/positive feedback.

Resource Name_____ Resource ISBN_____

Your Name_____ Your Position _____

School Name_____

Address _____

_____

Overall, what do you think about this resource ? _____

_____

_____

How does it help your students ?_____

_____

_____

What could you say to a colleague in a neighbouring school to persuade them to use this resource ?

_____

_____

How well does it match the specification and which specification is it ? _____

_____

Other Comments, suggestions for improvement, errors, please give the page number

_____

Resources I would like published

_____

Resources I might like to write, or have written, for consideration for publishing.

_____

Fax: 01745 826606 email: info@graham-lawler.com
post: Lawler Education, Lon Ffawydd/Beech Lane, Abergele LL22 7DY

Contents

Tutor Note Session One Singular and Plural Nouns	7
Singular and Plural Nouns	8
Spelling Plurals with -s or – es	9
Spelling Plurals with -s or -es 2	10
Tutor Notes Session Two Adding suffixes to verbs without changing the root word.	11
Adding suffixes to verbs without changing the root word.	12
Adding suffixes to verbs without changing the root word 2.	13
Adding suffixes to verbs without changing the root word 3.	14
Tutor Notes Session Three How the prefix un- changes the meaning of verbs and adjectives	15
How the prefix un- changes the meaning of verbs and adjectives	16
How the prefix un- changes the meaning of verbs and adjectives	17
How the prefix un- changes the meaning of verbs and adjectives	18
Tutor Notes Session Four Sentence construction as a combination of words.	19
Sentence construction as a combination of words.	20
More Sentence construction as a combination of words.	21
Making Sentences	22
Tutor Notes Session Five Joining Words and Clauses	23
Joining Words and Clauses	24
Joining Words and Clauses	25
Joining Words and Clauses	26
Teacher Notes Session Six Sequencing Sentences to Form Short Narratives.	27
Sequencing Sentences to Form Short Narratives.	28
Tutor Notes Session Seven Separation of Words with Spaces.	29
Separation of Words with Spaces	30
Tutor Notes Session Eight The Role of Capital Letters, Full stops/periods, question marks and exclamation marks to demarcate sentences.	31
The Role of Capital Letters, Full stops/periods, question marks and exclamation marks to demarcate sentences.	32
The Role of Capital Letters, Full stops/periods, question marks and exclamation marks to demarcate sentences	33
Capital Letters for Names and Personal Pronouns	34
More on Personal Pronouns	35

© 2018 Lawler Education. Teachers may copy these pages for use in their own school.

Tutor Notes Session One

Starter
We suggest you start the session by using the S1 powerpoint supplied with this book. It is a good ice breaker and should help students to focus in on basic plurals that they probably know anyway.

The students need to understand the definition of a noun and that if a word ends in -s, -sh, -ch, -x, or -z you add -es to make the plural form.
For almost all other nouns they need to add -s to make the plural form.

Main activity
Ask the students to complete the worksheets given with this session.

Plenary
To re-inforce the use of these rules ask questions that establish the plural forms, eg what is the plural for the following:

                    box ?
                    fox ?
                    skirt ?
                    shirt ?
                    church ?
                    push ?
                    change ?
                    dress ?
                    suit ?
                    shoe ?
                    car ?
                    house ?
                    bus ?
                    flower ?
                    shape ?

The purpose is to get the students looking at the last letter or letters and then to get used to applying the rules consistently. You may also want to mention local dialect. There may be circumstances in particular regions that stand out. We do know of one case in Liverpool where refugees were amused to discover that the local dialect for female partner is 'bird'.

© 2018 Lawler Education Teachers may copy these pages for use in their own school.

Singular and Plural Nouns   Name ....

This session is about 2 types of nouns.
A noun is a word that names something.
Singular nouns name only one thing.
Plural nouns name more than one thing.

Singular Noun: Names only 1 thing.   **Plural Noun:** Names more than 1 thing
Example   A daffodil   Example   Many daffodils

Put S against the single nouns and P against the plural nouns

S   P

Butterflies   Car   Cameras

Cars   Bus   Buses

© 2018 Lawler Education. Teachers may copy these pages for use in their own school.

Spelling Plurals with -s or -es

Name..

If a word ends in -s, -sh, -ch, -x, or -z you add -es to make the plural form.
For almost all other nouns you need to add -s to make the plural form.

Here is another example:

Maria waltz**es** with Josh on most Wednesday nights.

Look at these examples:

cross ⟶ cross**es**

catch ⟶ catch**es**

reach ⟶ reach**es**

push ⟶ push**es**

Try these

tax		car	
fax		glitz	
bush		frizz	
friend		publish	
shop		fish	
match		tractor	

Spelling Plurals with -s or -es 2   Name..

Try these

1   One car    Two _____

2   One Shape 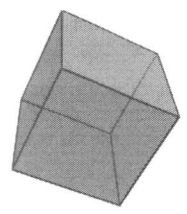   Many _____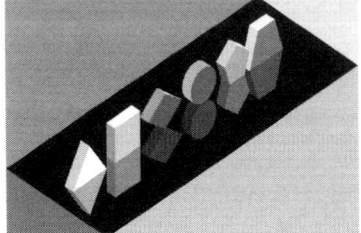

3   One church    Many _____

4   One puzzle    Many _____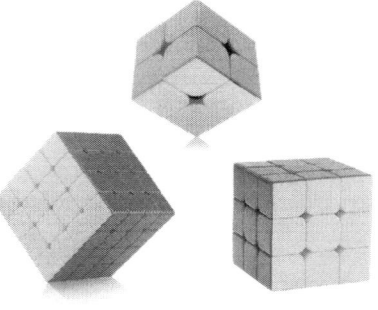

5   One jar    Many _____

Tutor Notes Session Two

Starter

Make sure students know what a suffix is and how it can be added to a word. Examples are -ed and -ing, eg played, playing. Use the powerpoint to 'warm up' the students.

There are also ODP versions on the disc associated with this book.

Main Activity

Talk through the worksheets with the students. In trials we found that some students were not aware of the meaning of the word coax but when defined they happily started to use it correctly.

Plenary

Ask the students to compare their answers with each other and ensure they have agreement. Then discuss the answers as a group.

Adding suffixes to verbs without changing the root word.

Name..

A suffix is an ending to a word. The word that the suffix is added to is called the root word. When you add - ed or -ing it changes the tense of the word.

Write the past tense by adding -ed   Write the present tense by adding -ing

talk		talk	
play		play	
walk		walk	
work		work	
sail		sail	

Circle the errors in these sentences and write the correct word on the line

1   Dave and I walking to college today. _____

2   I jumping for the header and scored the goal. _____

3   He is worked a late shift tonight. _____

4   I like plays tennis with Sarah. _____

5   Martha and her husband watching a film last night. _____

Adding suffixes to verbs without changing the Root Word 2   Name...

Remember a suffix is an ending to a word. The word that the suffix is added to is called the root word. When you add -ed or -ing it changes the tense of the word and the word changes from a verb to an adjective.

1. Complete the chart below with the correct -ed or -ing suffix.

Verb	to shift	to jump	to pump	to coax	to join	to peck	to mock
-ed	shifted						
-ing	shifting						

2 Complete the sentences below by inserting an adjective from this list so that the sentence makes sense.

shifting/shifted, jumped/jumping, pumping/pumped, coaxed/coaxing, joined/joining, pecked/pecking, mocked/mocking

a) Martin _____ all of the hurdles in the race. At this rate he will be a contender for the Olympics.

b) The fireman _____ the kitten down from the tree.

c) I hope to be _____ the college first team soon.

d) Ashok _____ iron for two hours in the gym.

e) Mary spent half an hour _____ Stella over the way Stella dressed. Mary was so mean.

3 Complete the chart below with the correct -ed or -ing suffix.

Verb	to alarm	to annoy	to astonish	to surround	to disappoint	to threaten	to interest
-ed							
-ing							

Adding suffixes to verbs
without changing the Root Word 3

Name. ....

Adjectives that end in -ing describe a person or thing that causes a particular feeling. For example, these flowers are very pleasing on the eye. This means they make people feel nice inside.

Choose the correct suffix, either -ed or -ing and fill in the gaps

1	The room was _____ when we heard the news.	buzz
2	We were _____ to hear that United lost the game.	amaze
3	Tanya _____ her muscles during the warm up for the game.	flex
4	Mike _____ fruit from the fruit bowl.	pick
5	The business is _____ by finance from the bank.	back
6	I am _____ the head office team for my new job.	join
7	Another word for being demanding is _____ .	tax
8	My dad _____ this land before me.	farm
9	The stolen car had been _____ in the lane.	abandon
10	Ben _____ the width of the entrance.	alter
11	Nisha _____ on stage in the musical.	appear
12	Nigel was _____ for a breach of the peace.	arrest
13	Bharat is _____ scones for the half-time break.	butter
14	Sima _____ the coin and won so we kicked off.	flip
15	Tom _____ his girlfriend's mum on her baking.	flatter

14   © 2018 Lawler Education. Teachers may copy these pages for use in their own school.

Tutor Notes Session Three

Starter

Use the powerpoint to stimulate discussion. It should make the students think. Make sure they understand that a prefix comes at the start of a word and that the suffix comes at the end of the word.
You may need to define an adjective and a verb and remind them of the definition of a noun.

Main Activity

Talk through the first worksheet with students and ask them to complete the sheet as you go along. They should then work on the second sheet on their own.
Keep asking questions to ask them to define a noun, adjective and verb at regular times throughout the session. This constant repetition will help them master the definitions for each type of word.

Plenary

Ask students to complete the last worksheet for this session. We suggest you end this session by emphasising that the prefix 'un' changes the meaning of the verb or adjective to the oppostite meaning.

How the prefix un- changes the meaning of verbs and adjectives eg unkind.

Name..

A prefix is added in front of a word to form a new word.
Think about what happens when you add a prefix like - un to words. What happens to the meaning of the original word ?

Think about the word kind and now add the prefix -un to it.
What happens to the meaning of the original word ?
Obviously the meaning is changed but did you notice the new meaning is the opposite to the original ?

Write the correct word in the blank, to complete the sentence.

unable, unwrap, untried, uninformed, undiagnosed, undelivered, unlikely, unimpressed, unsure, unimportant

1   Stella threw the information sheet in the bin. She felt it was _____.

2   Martin was _____ of the route.

3   Antonio had to _____ the meat before cooking it.

4   Imani has an illness the doctors cannot identify. The illness is _____.

5   Ashanti was seriously _____ by the show. She felt it was boring.

6   The parcel was listed as _____ .

7   Mike was _____ to join his wife, he had to work late.

8   Dina had to conduct experiments on the new _____ cereals, in the laboratory.

9   Parents were left, anxious, worried and _____.

10 Maaz was _____ to arrive on time, the traffic was so bad.

How the prefixes un- and dis changes the meaning of verbs and adjectives

Name ....

We now know that using the prefix - un changes the meaning of a verb or adjective to the opposite meaning. So the prefix -un means 'not'
Another prefix with the same meaning is 'dis'. Often 'dis ' is used as in to separate e.g disjoin or disable. These days 'un' and 'dis' are often interchangeable.

Write a single word with *dis* or *un* to complete each sentence.

1. My trainer is _____ .
   (not tied)

2. Imani _____ with Nisha.
   (does not agree)

3. Mark is _____ to beat Fred in tennis.
   (not able)

4. Mrs Chandarana does not want _____ painters working on her house.
   (not skilled)

5. Sarah is so _____ her desk is a mess.
   (not organised)

6. Martha's husband died yesterday and now she is so _____ .
   (not happy)

7. Charlotte _____the curtains, to hang them in her new home,
   (not folded)

8. Ebbe _____ mushroom soup.
   (not like)

How the prefixes un- and dis changes the meaning of verbs and adjectives 2

Name ....

Put the right prefix in front of the word to change the meaning to the opposite of what it means now.

| un | dis |

1 .... taste

2 .... clean

3 .... plug

4 .... screw

5 .... honest

6 .... wind

7 .... safe

8 .... well

9 ...... observed

10 .... sweetened

11 .... agree

12 ..... embark

13 ..... screw

14 ..... happy

15 ..... lucky

16 ....fasten

17 ......certain

18 ...... bolt

19 .....willing

20 ..... lodge

Tutor Notes Session Four

Starter

Inform the students that they are going to work with sentences in this session. It is important that they are aware of differing codes or registers of language. By this we mean the concept of adapting one's use of language.

For the purposes of this session they need to be aware that they are using more formal language and not necessarily the language used in casual situations between their contemporaries.

Main Activity

Read through page 20 with students and ask them to complete it as you go through it as a group.

The next activity we suggest is to ask them to form questions and to write the questions down on the board. Encourage then to look for patterns. We are looking for a recognition that questions start with what, where, why, when, who and how.
Now ask them to complete the 5 W's and an H worksheet on p 21.

Plenary

Ask the students to complete the 'Making Sentences ' on p22.

Sentence construction as a combination of words.

Name ....

A sentence is a collection of words that transmits meaning to another person.
The sentence can be spoken or written but must obey the rules of grammar. Most people agree that they prefer short clear sentences rather than rambling sentences.

The simplest sentences contain a subject and a verb (action word).
 For example in the sentence *Bharat yelled*, *Bharat* is the noun and *yelled* is the verb.

A sentence always starts with a capital letter and ends with a full stop.

These cards are mixed up. Write them in the right order to make a sentence.

1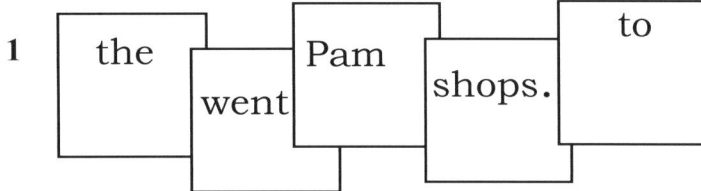

....

2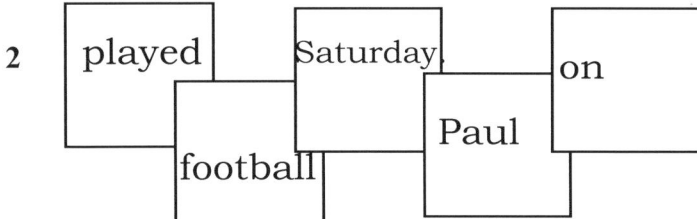

....

3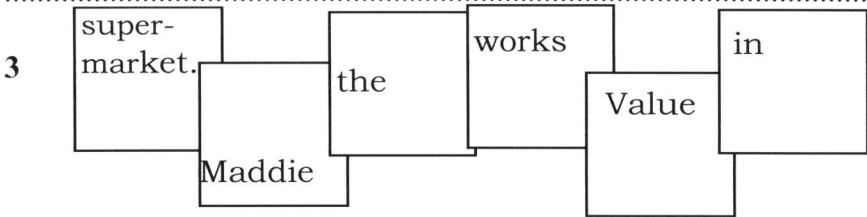

....

More Sentence Construction as a Combination of Words.   Name...

5 W's and an H

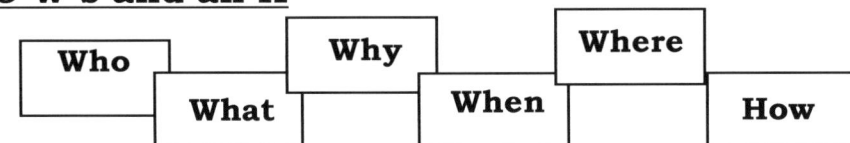

Add words to these sentences to answer the questions.

1 A _____ car crashed on the _____ .
     what ?   *where ?*

2 His older _____ is moving to _____ .
         who ?   *where ?*

3 The _____ dropped from _____ on _____ .
   who ?/ what ?   *where ?*   *when ?*

4 The _____ flowers in the _____ were _____ .
    what ?   *where ?*   *what ?*

5 Ashok played _____ brilliantly when we were at _____ .
    what ? / how ?   *where ?*

6 Sally watched _____ and _____ silently.
    what ? / how ?   *what ? / how ?*

7 The _____ police officer stopped _____ _____ .
    who ?   *where ?*   *why ?*

8 The _____ herded the _____ off the road to the _____ .
    who ?   *what ?*   *where ?*

9 The _____ had gone so the car was _____ started.
    what ?   *how ?*

10 Manish practised _____ everyday in his _____ .
     what ? / how ?   *where ?*

Making Sentences Name..

Put the words on the cards in the right order to make a clear sentence.

1

| these | sentence | Turn | cards | sensible | a | into |

2

| yesterday. | The | seen | was | car | red |

3

| farmer | Landrover. | his | blue | drove | The |

4

| ate | Thursday. | Matt | bagels | on | always |

5

| today. | The | arriving | boss | is | new |

Tutor Notes Session Five   Name..

Starter

Read through p 24 with the students and ensure they understand the role of joining words and clauses in a sentence.

Complete the worksheet as a group.

Now ask the students to identify as many joining words and clauses as they can and write them on the board.

Main Activity

Armed with this knowledge ask them to work through **Joining Words and Clauses 2.**

Plenary

For the plenary we have provided **Joining Words and Clauses 3,** alternatively you could ask them to prepare a powerpoint slide show on what they have learned.

Joining Words and Clauses

Name..

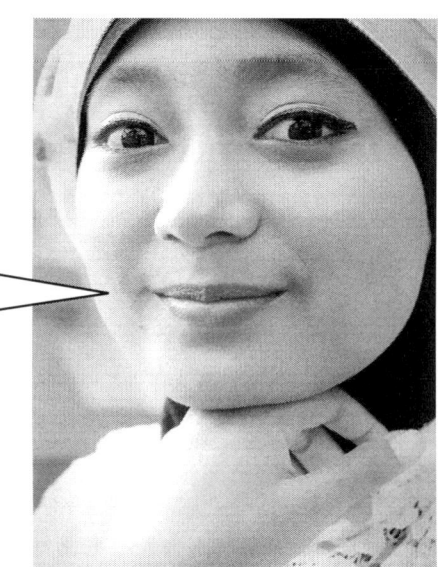

The word **and** is a very useful word. It is one of the words we can use to join sentences. There are other words like **if**, **or**, **but**, **so**, **until** and **whether**.
Look at the sentences on this worksheet and fill in the gaps with a joining word from the table. You may need to use some more than once.

| and | if | or | but | so | until | whether | to | in | because |

1 Marius drove to the college .... collect his wife.

2 My sister plays cricket in the summer .... she is really good.

3 Ashok is a late night radio dj .... he is allowed to sleep ..... every morning.

4 My husband won't start the car ....everyone has fastened their seat belt.

5 Kaleem asked Tahir ....he and his wife wished to join Kaleem and his wife for dinner.

6 Hamray is studying law .... that she can become a barrister ..... the future.

7 Michael was furious that he was booked by the police .... he was speeding.

8 Sarah was unsure .... to have fish .... a vegetarian meal in the restaurant.

9 Martin .... Sally have announced their engagement to marry.

10 Mary eats fruit everyday .... fruit helps you to have healthy skin and hair.

Joining Words and Clauses 2

Name..

O.K. now we need to step up the pace. What does this mean ? It means we are going to use the knowledge from earlier in this lesson to learn even more ways of joining sentences. Here we are going to link more sentences but using bigger words. Pick the best word from the list to fill in the gap.

otherwise, unless, in addition, in fact, moreover, although, instead, despite, therefore, however

1   Jonathan had to work .... of going out in the evening with his friends.

2   Petra had a part-time job .... to her day job in the dairy.

3   Peter passed his driving test .... only having two lessons.

4   Imini had to pay the bill .... the electricity company would cut them off.

5   .... you try to justify it, you lied to Nisha.

6   The car will not pass the M.O.T. .... you have a lot of work done to it.

7   .... Jason could not swim, he still jumped into the pool.

8   The company was bankrupt; .... the directors faced prison.

9   Anatoly could not take part ....Anatoly was quite drunk.

10 I did not get the letter; .... I was unable to answer it since it did not arrive.

Joining Words and Clauses 3   Name................................

O.K. by now you should be feeling much better with joining words and clauses. This worksheet has more words that you need to learn.
Don't worry, with practice it will become second nature for you.

Pick the best word from the list to fill in the gap.
You will not use every word in the list. and you may use some more than once.

Purpose words : So that, to, in order to.
Time words: When, while, after, until, since, as soon as.
Reason words: Because, as, since.
Contrast words: Although, but, in spite of.
Condition words: If, in case, unless, whether.

1	It rained a lot .... he still went out without a coat.

2	Fred reversed the car into the driveway .... it would be easier to unload the shopping.

3	Darren put himself on a diet .... look good for his wedding to Anna.

4	The delivery people were ready to go, ... the pizzas were cooked.

5	.... Mark had worked hard for the company he was still made redundant.

6	.... you want to do well in life you have to get qualified.

7	The new cooker will be fitted in the kitchen .... Ashok calls an electrician.

8	.... the delivery is late, I have organised a substitute.

9	We will be going at 4 o clock .... we need to arrive by half past five.

10	.... soon as Danisha arrives we will get started.

11	Kamran bought the new car .... travel to work by seven o clock in the morning.

12	.... the children were playing, Manisha enjoyed a cup of coffee.

13	I am not going out .... I have a terrible cold.

14	We won't move into London .... London homes are too expensive.

Teacher Notes Session Six

Starter

To prepare for this session you will need to print off copies of page 28 and cut them into strips.

Main Activity

Give the students an envelope of the strips and ask them to form a coherent story. There is information missing. Ask them what they can infer from the information they have been given.

Plenary

Tell the students this is an actual true story where scammers in Wales tricked people out of their money. It is worth telling the students that scammers approach their victims posing as police. They tell the victim that their help is needed because someone at the bank is stealing money. The victim is then asked to transfer their money to a safe bank account. In reality that account is controlled by the scammers who vanish with the victim's money.

The scammers warn the victim that people at the bank will ask questions and they are to avoid answering them because these are the people they are trying to catch. In reality the staff are trying desperately to help the victim making a major mistake. Some people in Wales lost substantial amounts of money. Make sure they know that the police will never involve a member of the public in an investigation.

Sequencing Sentences to Form Short Narratives.

This is an article from a local newspaper in Wales. It has been cut up into small sentences and they are in the wrong order.

Put them in order and then write an article to tell the story.

✂ ....

Victims are asked to take part to bring the culprits to justice.

✂ ....

Victims are told the money will be deposited back into their accounts afterwards, but they never see the money again.

✂ ....

When the victims hand over the money the crooks disappear.

✂ ....

The real Police will never ask you to be involved in a scam like this one.

✂ ....

Crooks claim to be investigating a local bank branch fraud where staff are suspected of being involved.

✂ ....

Victims are told to get their money out and hand it over where it will be put into a 'safe' account.

✂ ....

This is a true story, it really did happen.

Tutor Notes Session Seven

Starter

Introduce the concept of white space as the absence of text on the page. Students need to understand that the readability of text is affected by what we call 'white space' but students also need to understand that the space does not have to be white.

Main Activity

Ask students to design a web page for the college website or for a personal website. They should do this in MS word or another suitable software programme. They need to ensure they use the white space to improve the readability of their text.

Plenary

Ask the students to work through the worksheet on page 30.

Separation of Words with Spaces.   Name..

Words are separated with spaces to make reading easier. Originally stories were told out loud because most people could not read. It became important to separate words to help people to read silently. There is a man called Paul Saenger who has written a book about how silent reading started and it started in the British Isles and spread around the world.

Spaces between words are important because they help us to read. These spaces are where the punctuation is put. These are the rules to help us read clearly.

Uisng the audio app on your phone, read and record the following paragraph.

Detectivechief inspector JohnMundela walked into the roomand pausedhelookedaround where isHamiltonheasked Policeconstablekateswannsaid notsuresir hetookacallearlierandranfromthebuilding Mundelatookhisphonefromhispocketand dialledquicklyandwaitedwhereareyouman Hamiltonwasbreathlesshe said sir IhavealeadontheAprilcarter case wemissedavitalclueanditwassitting rightunderournoses.

Rewrite the paragraph with punctuation and spaces between the words.

_____
_____
_____
_____
_____
_____

Now re-record the story using your newly written article. Which version do you perefer ?

_____
_____

Tutor Notes Session Eight   Name..

Starter

Review the lessons learned from the last session on the use of white space. We suggest that you stress that sentences always start with a capital letter and end with a full stop. They also need to know that the term ' full stop' is British English but 'period' is American English. They also need to know that these terms are used to show that a matter is settled.

'The matter is closed. Full stop.'

or

'The matter is closed. Period.'

Main Activity

You will need to explain the role of question marks and exclamation marks and personal pronouns.
Work through p 33 and 34 with students as a group.

Plenary

If they need more practice, use p 32 and p 35.

Capital Letters, full stops/periods, question marks and exclamation marks to demarcate sentences.

Name..

Sentences always start with a capital letter and end with a full stop. You will find some people call full stops 'periods'. They are the same thing, they show when a sentence ends. As well as this, question marks show when a question has been asked and ...

... exclamation marks give a word more strength and add a sense of urgency. They can be used to show someone is shouting.

Punctuation rules help reading because they are rules to help us understand what the author meant. Rewrite these sentences and put in punctuation to make them read well.

1 martha was lookingforward to dinner with her husband bill

....

2 thewaythings aregoing we will be here for a month of sundays

....

3 if I have saidthis once Ihavesaiditonethousandtimes

....

4 you did a terrificjob

....

5 theteamwere fantasticwhat a greatgame

....

Capital Letters, full stops/periods, question marks and exclamation marks to demarcate sentences 2   Name..

Rewrite these sentences with a capital letter, a question mark or exclamation mark, a full stop/period and spaces to ensure they read well.

1   whattimeis the championshipmatch

....

2   welldone harry

....

3   whydid nigel avoidgoingto those meetings

....

4   whyare all of thesemeetings required

....

5   congratulations youhavepassed your driving test

....

6   canyouremember where you last saw it

....

7   whyare we leavingat this early hour

....

8   can you pickme up from work later

....

9   whatis the time

....

10   canwe have spaghetti bolognese

....

Capital Letters for Names and Personal Pronouns   Name......................

Remember a noun is the name of a person or thing. A pronoun is a word that is used in place of a noun. So for instance we could say ' Kate went to the shop.' But the next sentence would say ' She' rather than repeating Kate's name. 'She' is the pronoun.

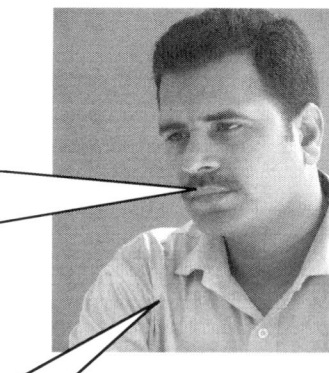

Rewrite each sentence and:
1. Make sure that the sentence starts with a capital letter and,
2 Change the underlined word or words to a pronoun.

Some popular pronouns: I, you, he, she, it, we, they, you, him, her, them, us.

1   satish made dinner for the whole family.

_____

2   paul played tennis with Sarah. Later Paul and Sarah went to the cinema.

_____

3   mr Jones said hello to Mrs Jones.

_____

4   the bungalow needs re-painting. The bungalow has flaky paint work.

_____

5   the car broke down, the car needs a new clutch.

_____

More on Personal Pronouns

Name..

Circle the pronouns in the sentences below. Some sentences have more than one pronoun.

1   She went to the shop with Nisha.

2   When it is raining he takes an umbrella with him to work.

3   Andre always eats chips on a Thursday; he likes them after playing snooker.

4   Have you hung the painting on the wall yet?

5   I enjoyed seeing them again but I was glad to see them go.

6   She paid for her petrol with a twenty pound note and then the cashier gave her change.

7   Mark is booked to be here in one hour to fix the leak; he had better be on time.

8   What does she see in him?

9   I sent her the email but it bounced back.

10   We played with the puppy, then we fed him a biscuit.

Interactive White Board Activities 1

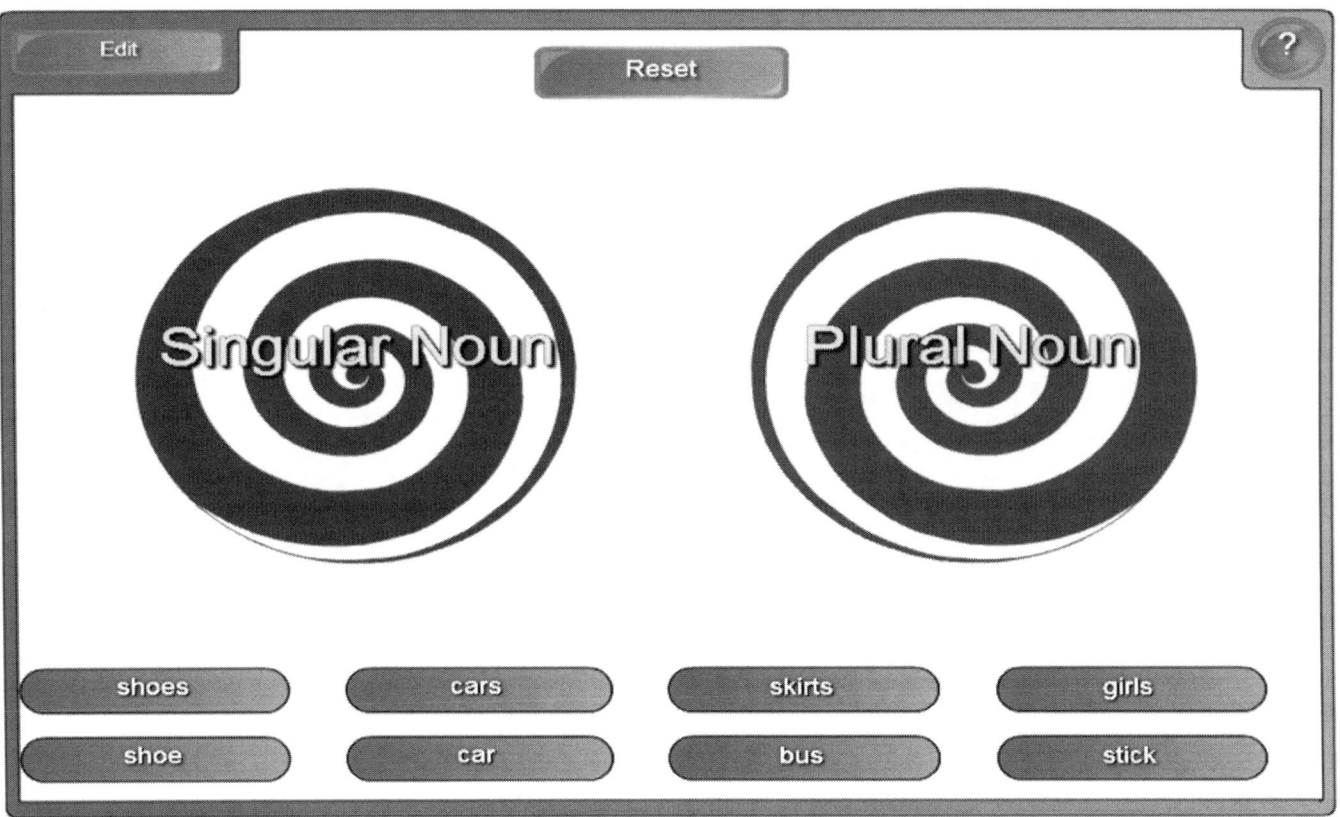

This is a vortex. The idea here is that the students drag the words by using their finger, to the correct vortex. If they are right it will swallow the word. If they are wrong it will fling it back at them.

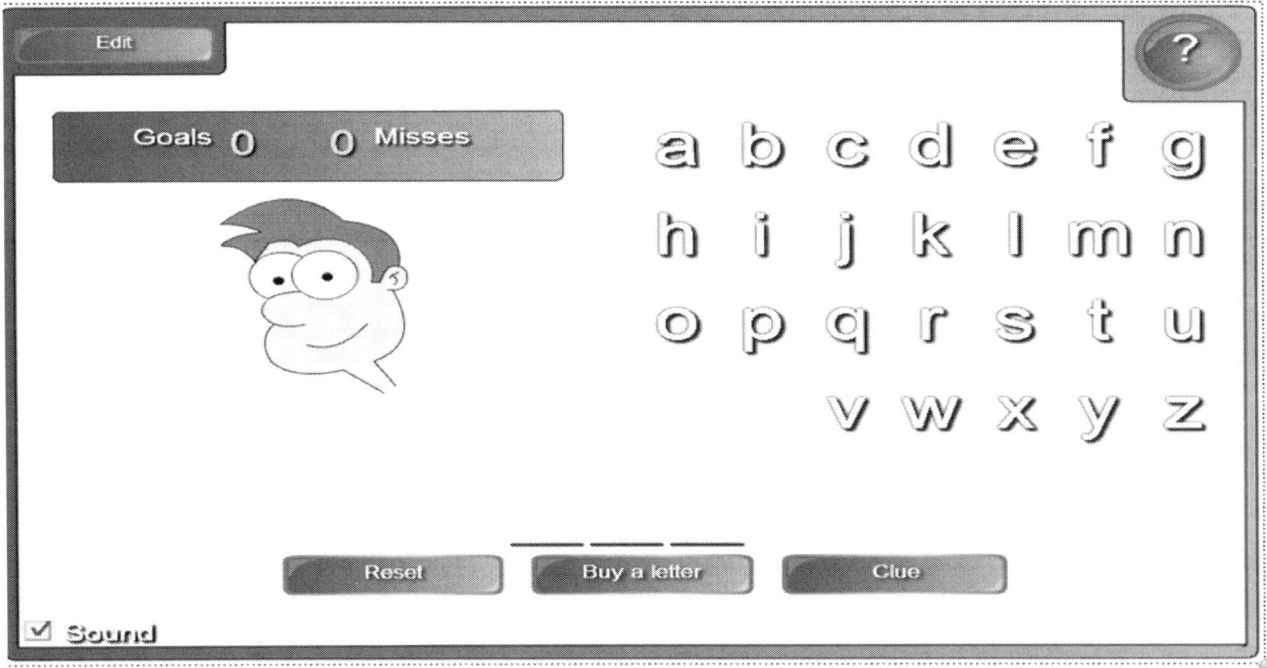

This is tomato splat. The students click on clue and then have to work out the word that the clue refers to. They then click on the letters to spell the word. If they are right, the cartoon gets splatted with a tomato.

Interactive White Board Activities 2

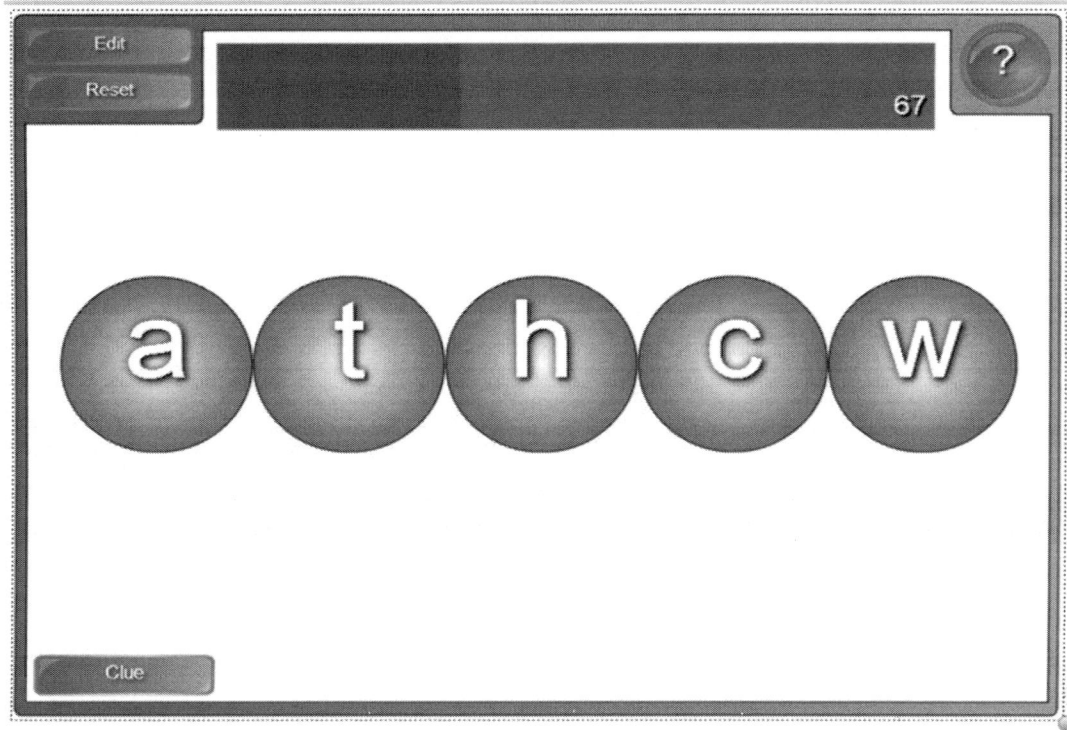

This is an anagram. The students need click on the clue and then determine the word. They then have to drag the balls by hand to make the word and they are against the clock. There are three versions of this activity, fast, medium and slow. Professional judgement is needed to determine the most appropriate version.

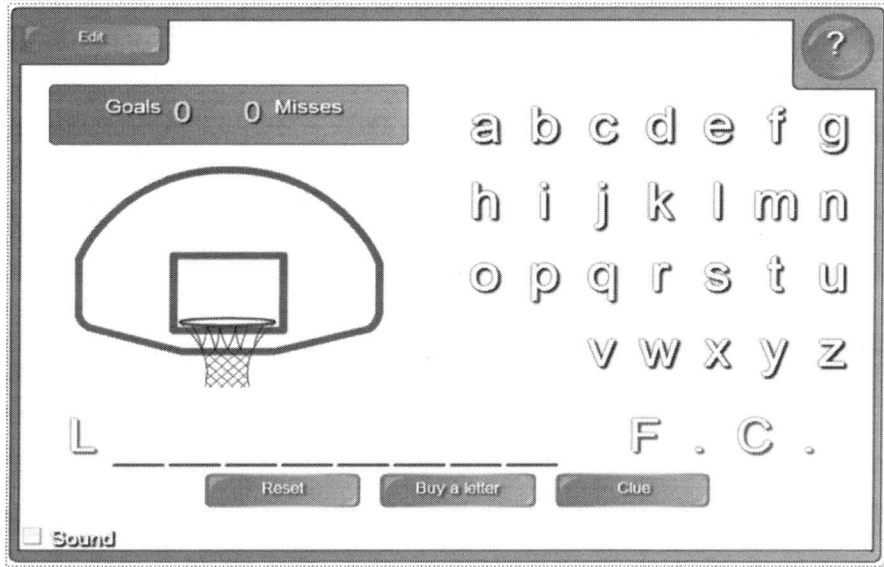

This is the same as Tomato splat above but this time it is shooting basketballs. The students click on the clue and then have to spell the word. They then shoot a basket. It is fun, HONESTLY!

Other Titles from Lawler Education

Skills for Literacy 2   9781842854563 **Dr Susan Young**

This book covers:
- the formation of nouns using suffixes like -ness, -er and by compounding eg superman, whiteboard.
- the formation of adjectives using suffixes such as -ful, -less.
- the use of suffixes, -er, est in adjectives (e.g. faster, fastest) and the use of -ly to turn adjectives into adverbs such as bad and badly, slow and slowly, careful.
- subordination, using when, if, that because and co-ordination using or and but.
- expanding noun phrases for description and specification eg the blue butterfly, self-raising flour, the big tractor.
- how grammatical patterns in a sentence indicate its function as a statement, question, exclamation or command.

Skills for Literacy 3   9781842854570 **Dr Susan Young**

his book covers:
- using the correct tense (present/past) consistently throughout writing.
- use the progressive form of verbs in the present and past tense to mark actions in progress eg she was shouting.
- use of capital letters, full stops, question marks and exclamation marks in punctuation.
- the use of commas to separate items in a list.
- the correct use of apostrophes.

Skills for Literacy 4   9781842854587 **Dr Susan Young**

This book covers:
- using the correct tense (present/past) consistently throughout writing.
- use the progressive form of verbs in the present and past tense to mark actions in progress eg she was shouting.
- use of capital letters, full stops, question marks and exclamation marks in punctuation.
- the use of commas to separate items in a list.
- the correct use of apostrophes.

Skills for Literacy 5   9781842854594 **Dr Susan Young**

This book covers:
- the formation of nouns using a range of prefixes (eg super, anti, auto)
- the use of the forms *a* or *an* according to whether the next word begins with a vowel or a consonant.
- word families based on common words showing how words are related in form and meaning (eg solve, solution, solver, dissolve, insoluble).
- how to express time, place and cause using conjunctions, (eg when , before, after, while, so because).
- adverbs (eg then, next, soon, therefore) or prepositions (before, after, during, in, because, of)

Other Titles from Lawler Education

Skills for Literacy 6   9781842854600 **Dr Susan Young**
This book covers:
- the use of paragraphs as a way of grouping related material.
- the use of the perfect form of verbs instead of the simple past.
- the use of inverted commas to punctuate direct speech.
- the grammatical difference between the plural and possessive -s.
- standard English forms for verb inflections instead of locally spoken forms.
- noun phrases expanded by the addition of modifying adjectives, nouns and preposition phrases.
- fronted adverbials.
- use of paragraphs to organise ideas around a theme.
- to indicate parentheses,

Skills for Literacy 7   9781842854617 **Dr Susan Young**
This book covers:
- the appropriate choice of pronoun or noun within and across sentences to aid comprehension and avoid repetition.
- the use of inverted commas.
- apostrophes to mark plural possession.
- the use of commas on fronted adverbials.
- the use of brackets, dashes or commas
- the difference between vocabulary typical of informal speech and that which is appropriate for formal speech and writing eg find out, discover, ask for, request.

Skills for Literacy 8   9781842854624 **Dr Susan Young**
This book covers
- how words are related by meanings as synonyms and antonyms.
- The use of the passive to affect the presentation of information in a sentence
- The difference between informal and formal speech structures.
- linking ideas across paragraphs using a wide range of cohesive devices.
- repetition of words or phrases.
- grammatical connections.
- ellipsis.
- the use of the semi-colon, colon and dash.
- the use of hyphens to avoid ambiguity.

Entry Level: Whole Numbers 978-1-84285-439-6 **Dr Edward G. James**

The 'beating heart' of this book is the belief that all can learn. Dr James has worked in schools and colleges for many years and has many years experience of teaching learning limited students who are classed as ALN/SEN.

The book comes with teacher support notes and powerpoint slide shows to help teachers to teach.

There are also some basic interactive white board exercises that engage children in their learning.

Other Titles from Lawler Education

Application of Number: Motor Vehicle Mechanics: Stock Control
978-1-84285-448-8 **Andy Burns**

This book is a series of lessons with activities for teachers covering functional skills/ Essential Skills Wales/ Core Skills Scotland Application of Number.

The lessons provide a scenario where students have to engage in stock control. The actual numeracy being delivered is the use of percentages, decimals and fractions. It is essential that this cohort of students can work comfortably within each of these basic skill areas and can switch when required. The contextualisation of these skills within the motor vehicle trade motivates them to learn since they are given a purpose.

Skills for Life   978-1-84285-416-7 **Judith Parfitt**

This book covers:
- Asking Questions
- How do you ?
- Getting Around Town
- Using the Telephone
- Small Talk
- Vocabulary Busters
- Starting to Talk
- Asking Tough Questions.

More Skills for Life 978-1-84285-419-8 **Judith Parfitt**

This book is an extension of the highly successful Skills for Life now in its second edition. In this book we concentrate on developing the language skills and understanding of the student by developing their language in situations inside and around their home and locality.

This book also comes with free Smartboard activities and free audio files to help poor English readers.

Department Store Maths   Dr Edward G James 978-1-84285-453-2
Contents:
What's the cost? Dept Store Vocabulary, Go Figure!
Can you buy any of these? What is the total cost?
Dept Store Employees, Making Change, What would you do? Paying the Docket, What item will you buy?
Comparing costs, calculating percentages, how short are you?
Chart the Items, Chart the Purchase, The Regular Price, Your Savings, Shopping for Christmas,
Your own shopping Spree, Your Own Departmental Store,
Europe and the Euro,
Setting up home